April in the Arctic.
Snow clouds still scuttle across the sky.
Temperatures barely nudge above freezing.
But every now and again,
    the clouds part,
        the sun shines,
            and the frozen world stretches awake.

A black nose pokes from a snow bank.
Curious eyes blink in the brightness.
It is a mother polar bear,
        crawling from her den,
            seeing her world for the first time in five months.
For all that time, she has been in the den she dug beneath the snow.
        Not eating.
        Never leaving.
        Surviving on her stored fat.
        For the first month, she waited for her babies' birth.
        For the next four,
            she nursed them,
                nestled them,
                    kept them safe and warm.
They grew . . .
        from two pounds to twenty-two,
            from toothless to sharp-toothed,
                from downy-haired to densely furred.
But as the babies got bigger,
        Mother grew thinner.
Now the cubs are ready to meet the outside world.

And Mother needs to go home,
      to the ice,
            to hunt and eat and survive.
She drags herself from the cramped den.
She shakes and stretches and rolls in the snow.
      Then she stands,
      scans the distance,
      sniffs the air.
Is it safe?
It is.
She calls to her cubs.

CANDACE FLEMING   ERIC ROHMANN

POLAR BEAR

To Nora—
Grrr!
Candace Fleming
2023

NEAL PORTER BOOKS
HOLIDAY HOUSE/NEW YORK

Two little bears—one female, one male—tumble from the den.

Bleating and squealing, they scramble onto their mother.

This new, outside world is scary.

Mother chuffs softly and nurses them in the sun.

Soon, they will return to the familiar comfort of their den.

But the next day they venture out again.

And the day after that.

And the day after that.

Mother is getting her cubs used to the outdoors,

to the cold,

and the blowing snow.

The cubs wrestle.

They play.

Their muscles get stronger.

On the seventh day, Mother's instinct tells her it's time.

She nudges the cubs away from the only place they have known.

One cub whimpers.

The other squalls.

Where are they going?

Home to the ice.

Mother knows the way by heart,

along a trail she took with her own mother,

along a trail she took as a mother-to-be,

along a trail her cubs will take when they are grown,

across frozen ponds,

and slippery ridges,

and gullies filled with powder-fresh snow.

Grown bears can walk fifty miles a day.

But not babies.

Their tiny legs tire quickly.

"Aruuu!" they cry.

Mother stops and snuggles them in to nurse and nap.

But soon they are walking again.

Suddenly, Mother stops. Sniffs. Stands.

Two wolves are circling for an attack.

Mother grunts for the cubs to keep close.

The wolves inch nearer.

"Aruuuu!" cry the babies. They are too small to run.

And Mother will never leave them.

Hissing, she rises up to her full height—all seven feet of her.

She is huge.

Fierce.

She growls.

The wolves stop. Look. Lope away.

But Mother takes no chances. She keeps the babies moving.

Following her nose.

Following her instincts.

For forty miles.

And still she has not eaten.

On the sixth day of their journey, they come to the shore.

Just like their mother, the cubs stop, sniff, stand.

Their tiny nostrils fill with the scent of sea salt.

     It is the smell of the ice-covered Hudson Bay.

       It is the smell of home.

The family heads out across the fractured ice.

     Mother striding.

     The cubs slipping.

The little ones sense a change in their mother.
Her nose picks up every scent on the breeze.
Her feet feel every vibration in the ice.
Her ears hear the faintest of sounds.
The cubs have never seen her act like this before.
What is she looking for?

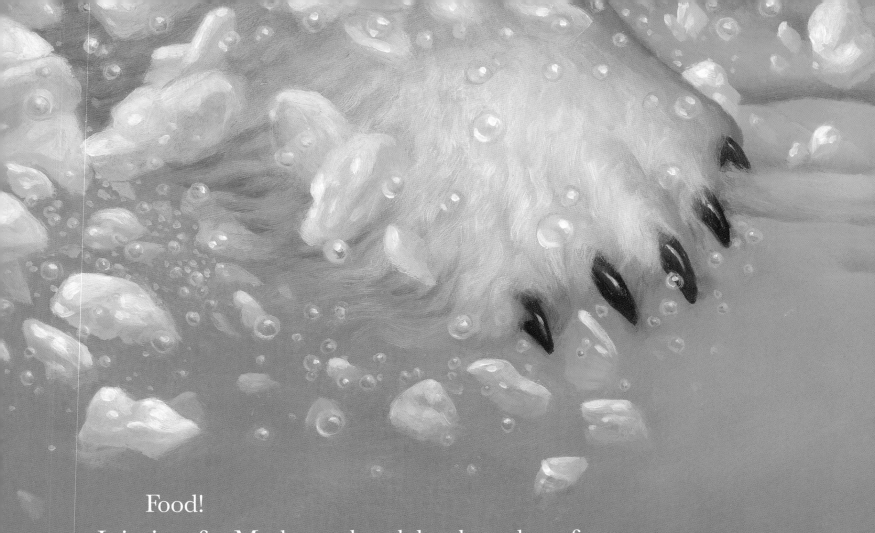

Food!
It is time for Mother to break her long, long fast.
The ice is the polar bear's hunting ground. And springtime on the
ice is the best time to catch her favorite meal: a ringed seal.
      Stop . . .
            sniff . . .
      Yes!
Mother has found a seal's breathing hole.
      She stills,
            stiffens,
                  listens.
Seals must take a breath every thirty minutes.
Mother waits.

So does the female cub.
She copies her mother,
    crouching,
        watching,
            getting her first lesson in hunting.
Someday she will grow up to feed cubs of her own.
Huff!
Air puffs through the hole.
    Mother rises up,
        crashes down,
            smashes through snow and the ice-crusted dome
of the breathing hole.
Her claws grasp at . . .
    Nothing!
Only one in ten hunts succeed.
Mother's stomach rumbles.
No meal today.

But over the next days and weeks, Mother hunts hard, while the cubs watch and learn.

They sniff where she sniffs.

They look where she looks.

They lie down and wait patiently when she stalks prey.

Ahhhh!

They taste the reward of rich seal blubber.

By the start of June, the bear family has moved far out onto the ice. The cubs are growing fast—very fast.

And Mother has gorged herself. She has regained much of her weight. But it is not enough.

Soon, the bay's ice will melt into open water.

And seals are almost impossible to catch in open water.

Mother must fatten up now if she and the cubs are to survive summer's lean months.

Already there are meltwater pools on the surface of the ice. And the late spring sun feels warmer than Mother remembers. It has always been hard to live on the ice.

Unpredictable weather has made it even harder.

Too much ice is melting too soon.

And too little ice means too little food.

Mother moves the family to the edge of the ice in hopes of
catching one last meal.

Snaaap!

The ice breaks off and is carried out,

    far out,

        into open water.

Mother stops, sniffs, stands.

Nothing is familiar.

Not the smell of the air.

Not the feel of the ice.

For the first time in her life, she does not know where she is.

What has happened to the Arctic spring world she has
always known?

All she can see is water.

    All the way to the horizon.

Mother's instinct tells her they must swim for shore.

Adult bears can swim sixty miles nonstop.

But not young cubs.

Can they survive?

They have no choice.
Mother slips into the Arctic water.
She calls to her cubs to follow.
Under the golden glow of twenty-four hour
daylight, they swim and swim.
An hour passes.
    Two.
        Three.

The cubs struggle to keep up.
They struggle to hold their heads above water.
They cry and grab at their mother.
Hungry.
Tired.
Cold.

How much farther?
Four hours.
Five.
Mother lifts her nose.

She sniffs the air.
She smells land even if she cannot see it.
She circles around the cubs, nudging at them to keep swimming.
But the cubs are cold.
    So cold.
A shelf of ice suddenly looms before them.
They have to climb, but the cubs cannot.
Mother is tired, too. Still, she pushes first one dripping cub
from the sea, and then the second.
The cubs shiver on the ice.
Mother presses them to her belly.
    They are too tired to nurse.
    They are too tired to cry.
As Mother's heat radiates through them, they fall asleep.

It is July, and lakes that were frozen just days before
suddenly teem with birds from the south.
Wildflowers speckle the tundra.
Insects buzz and bite.
It is hard for polar bears to survive without ice.
Mother lives mostly on her fat stores.
The babies live mostly on her milk.
And still they grow.
To conserve energy, they amble in the cool of early
morning and late afternoon,
     rest at mid-day,
          sleep through the night.
They are waiting for the return of the ice.
They are waiting for home.

But cubs will be cubs.
They bite each other,
    cuff,
        roll around.
They weigh almost a hundred pounds now,
but still act like babies.

In September, the frost returns; birds fly away.

The days grow dark, and an early snow sweeps across the tundra.

Mother knows it is time to meet the ice.

They walk north,

    along the coast,

        in search of an early freeze.

By mid-October, they are there.

So are lots of other polar bears.

Waiting.

All waiting.

For solid ice to form and their home to return.

Mother, like all the others, is eager to hunt.

Slowly, skirts of ice form around boulders.

A frozen skin spreads across the black water.

But it is taking so long.

    Too long.

Mother knows this in her genes. It is past time to return to the ice.

Hunger gnaws at her. The layer of fat needed to sustain her cubs
is disappearing. Summer has taken its toll.

She desperately needs seal blubber.

She desperately needs to eat.

Finally, a deep cold rolls in.
Ice crystals form on the bay's surface.
Tendrils of ice bind and solidify the water.
Mother tests its thickness.
        Craaack!
Not yet.
She nibbles on kelp,
        impatient,
                hungry,
                        until . . .
                                at last . . .

Hudson Bay in December is an unbroken white vista
stretching to the horizon.
Home!
But the year-old cubs have never known the ice in winter.
It is a time of slashing snow, and whipping winds,
        of deep, deep cold,
                and twenty-four-hour darkness.
This first winter, they will stay close to their mother,
        hunting more,
                nursing less,
                        growing in size and strength.
Spring will return . . . then summer . . . then fall.
And then . . . a second winter, and the cubs will separate,
first from their mother,
        then from each other.
Each bear will walk on,
        alone,
beneath the Arctic sky,
        along familiar paths,
                at home on the ice.

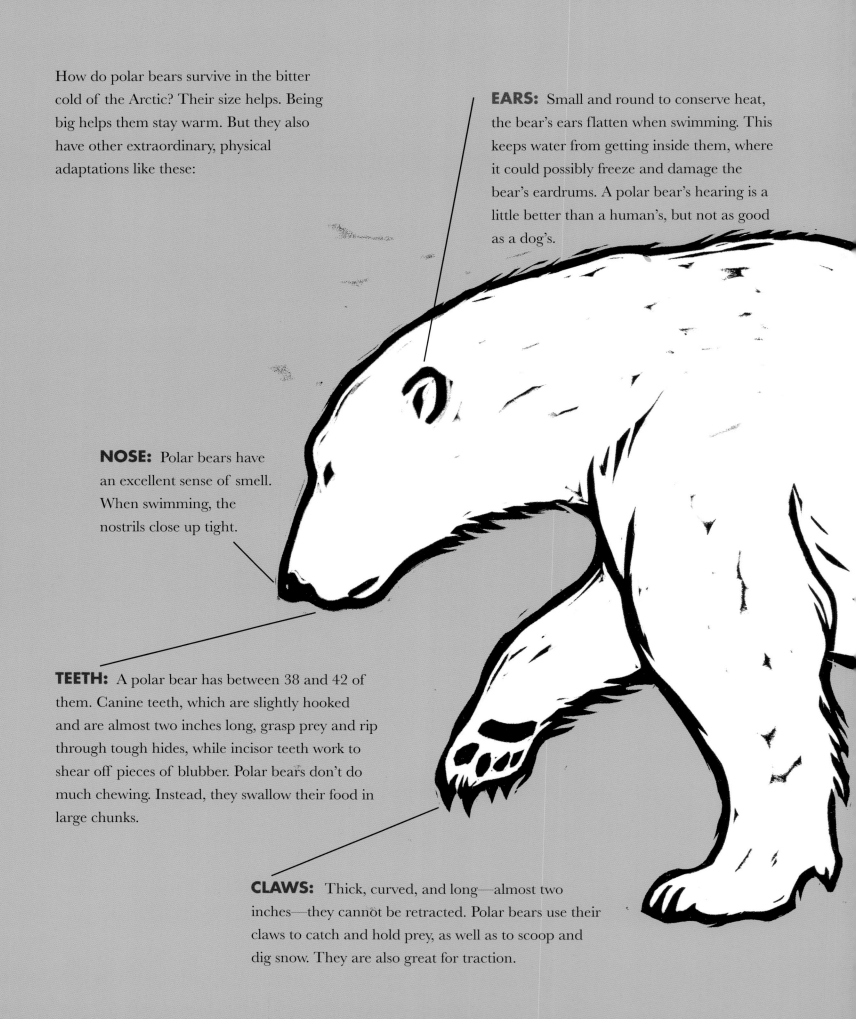

How do polar bears survive in the bitter cold of the Arctic? Their size helps. Being big helps them stay warm. But they also have other extraordinary, physical adaptations like these:

EARS: Small and round to conserve heat, the bear's ears flatten when swimming. This keeps water from getting inside them, where it could possibly freeze and damage the bear's eardrums. A polar bear's hearing is a little better than a human's, but not as good as a dog's.

NOSE: Polar bears have an excellent sense of smell. When swimming, the nostrils close up tight.

TEETH: A polar bear has between 38 and 42 of them. Canine teeth, which are slightly hooked and are almost two inches long, grasp prey and rip through tough hides, while incisor teeth work to shear off pieces of blubber. Polar bears don't do much chewing. Instead, they swallow their food in large chunks.

CLAWS: Thick, curved, and long—almost two inches—they cannot be retracted. Polar bears use their claws to catch and hold prey, as well as to scoop and dig snow. They are also great for traction.

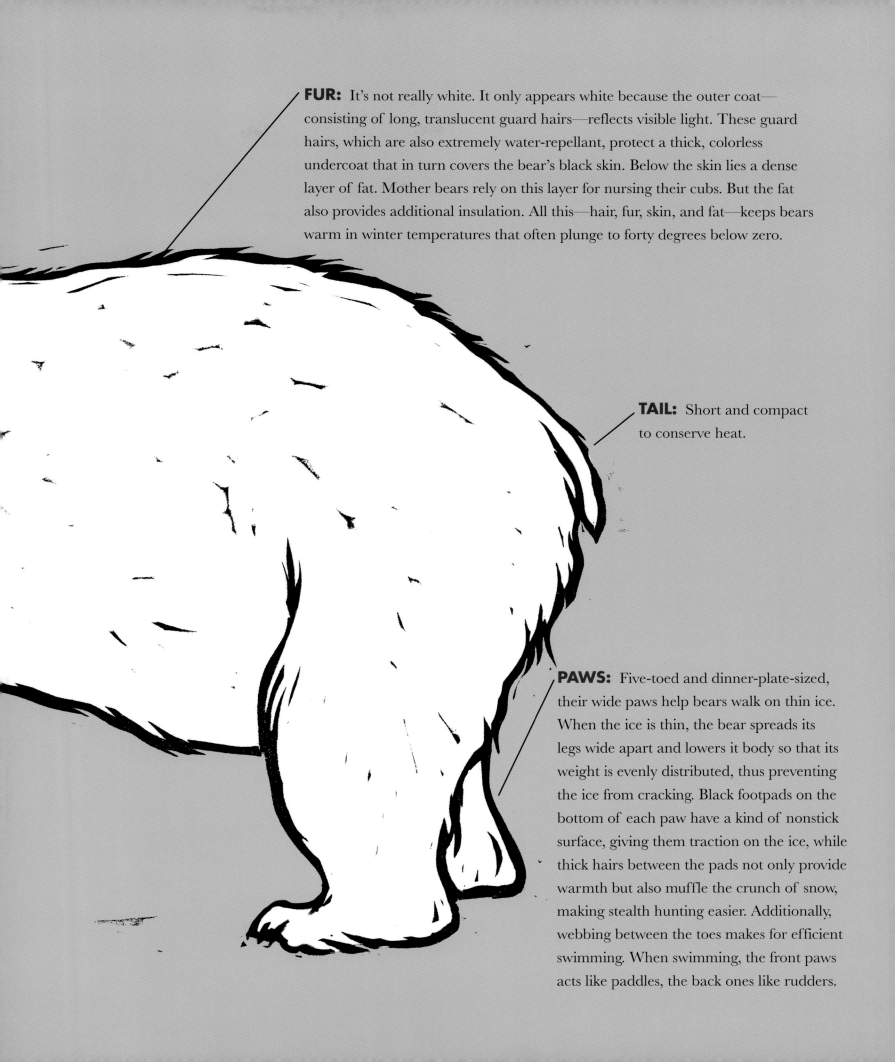

FUR: It's not really white. It only appears white because the outer coat—consisting of long, translucent guard hairs—reflects visible light. These guard hairs, which are also extremely water-repellant, protect a thick, colorless undercoat that in turn covers the bear's black skin. Below the skin lies a dense layer of fat. Mother bears rely on this layer for nursing their cubs. But the fat also provides additional insulation. All this—hair, fur, skin, and fat—keeps bears warm in winter temperatures that often plunge to forty degrees below zero.

TAIL: Short and compact to conserve heat.

PAWS: Five-toed and dinner-plate-sized, their wide paws help bears walk on thin ice. When the ice is thin, the bear spreads its legs wide apart and lowers it body so that its weight is evenly distributed, thus preventing the ice from cracking. Black footpads on the bottom of each paw have a kind of nonstick surface, giving them traction on the ice, while thick hairs between the pads not only provide warmth but also muffle the crunch of snow, making stealth hunting easier. Additionally, webbing between the toes makes for efficient swimming. When swimming, the front paws acts like paddles, the back ones like rudders.

IT'S ALL ABOUT THE ICE

We share our planet with something like 26,000 polar bears. Found in nineteen populations across the Arctic, these powerful, majestic animals amble along the coasts of five nations: the United States (Alaska), Canada, Russia, Greenland, and Norway (Svalbard). Science calls them *Ursus maritimus*, meaning "sea bear" in Latin. But it is sea *ice* that they depend on.

Polar bears, or at least their tracks, have been found almost as far north as the pole. Some bears live on the frigid, year-round sea ice of Kane Basin in Greenland. Others trace the frozen coastline of the remote Chukchi Sea, a waterway between Russia and Alaska. The bears in this story, however, make their home farther south in Canada's Western Hudson Bay area.

From overhead, Hudson Bay looks like a giant paw print. It is actually a vast inland sea, shallow and almost completely surrounded by land. Every summer the bay's ice disappears completely. The Hudson Bay bears move with this ice, hunting seals through the winter and into the summer (November to mid-July). Seal blubber is the perfect food: nutrient-rich and high in fat and calories. And in the spring and early summer, the Hudson Bay is a polar buffet. The bears hunt intensively. They eat and eat. They get fatter and fatter. Finally, when the last of the ice melts close to the shore, the bears clamber onto land. Food is scarce there. After all, birds, eggs, and berries cannot sustain an animal that weights up to 1,400 pounds. And so the bears will live off their stored body fat until the return of winter ice. Most bears go without eating for about four to five months. For every day they don't eat, they lose two pounds! As for expectant mothers, they remain on land to give birth, and go without food for about eight months. This prolonged fasting is not a problem. Bears *can* survive . . . if they have plenty of fat stored.

But the Arctic is warming. Sea ice is melting. And on Hudson Bay, the time bears have to hunt and build up their body condition has been cut short. The time they're forced to go without eating has lengthened. Why? Because the ice there is melting three and a half weeks earlier and freezing three and a half weeks later. Studies have shown that for each week earlier the ice breaks up, Hudson Bay bears come ashore twenty-two pounds lighter. This means they may not have enough fat stores to survive their summer fast. They may not be able to reproduce, nurse their cubs, stay warm during the winter months, or fight off diseases.

Less ice also means more open water. Bears are being forced to swim farther and farther to find a meal, to reach ice, or to get to shore. And while polar bears are excellent swimmers, paddling long distances through frigid water uses up those essential stores of body fat. Oftentimes, the energy and fat used to catch a meal exceeds the calories eventually consumed. The result is thinner, less healthy bears.

Loss of this sea ice habitat has affected seals, too. Fewer seal pups are being born in the Hudson Bay, and the adults are smaller. Since polar bears rely almost exclusively on a calorie-loaded diet of seals, a shortage of this prey will have a dire effect.

Sadly, the bears living in Western Hudson Bay aren't the only ones affected by this warming. Polar bears across the entire Arctic, even those in Greenland's frigid Kane Basin, are experiencing an earlier ice melt and later ice growth. They, too, are being forced ashore earlier, and fasting longer.

Why is this happening?

It's because of human-caused climate change. Most of our energy comes from fossil fuels—coal, oil, natural gas. When we burn these fossils, we pump huge amounts of carbon dioxide into the Earth's atmosphere. Normal amounts of carbon dioxide in the atmosphere act like a blanket, trapping heat and keeping our planet at a stable temperature. But we are adding way too much carbon dioxide to the atmosphere. This buildup of carbon dioxide thickens the blanket, trapping too much heat. Too much heat causes rising global temperatures, which in turn melt Arctic ice.

But there is hope. We can save sea ice and help polar bears survive by changing our behavior in very simple ways. We can reduce our energy consumption by walking, biking, carpooling or taking public transportation. We can turn off lights, and lower the thermostats in our homes. "If everybody did those things, it would be a start," says Dr. Andrew Derocher, a biological scientist at the University of Alberta at Edmonton. Additionally, we can talk with our families, teachers, and community leaders about polar-bear-friendly energy sources like solar, wind, and water. We can talk about climate change and climate solutions. Above all, we can inspire those around us to care. Caring, after all, is the first step toward significant change.

A FEW COOL FACTS

1. The polar bear is the "apex predator" of the Arctic. It has no natural enemy that seeks it as prey.

2. Polar bears can run as fast as a galloping horse—thirty miles an hour—but only for a short distance. That's because they overheat easily (imagine sprinting in a thick, fur-lined parka). Instead, polar bears prefer to amble along at a speed of three miles an hour.

3. Young bears are not astute hunters when first left on their own. Instead, they often follow other bears' tracks, adopting a simple rule: where other polar bears are, there may be food. It is common for young bears to survive by eating remains of kills made by adult bears.

4. Polar bears don't hydrate just by drinking water. They get a portion of their water from a chemical reaction that breaks down fat—another reason for them to gobble seal blubber. They do eat snow in the winter, however, and in the summer they drink fresh water.

5. While polar bears are typically loners, sometimes they will hang out together while consuming a big meal like a whale carcass, or while waiting for the ice to freeze. A group of polar bears is called a sleuth, and males will play-fight with each other. They can recognize friends they've met before even if they haven't encountered each other in years.

6. An average female polar bear will have up to six litters during her lifetime (typically twenty to twenty-five years). From about the age of five, females produce cubs approximately every three years until they reach their twenties. The oldest recorded mother bear was twenty-eight when she gave birth to cubs. While most litters are twins, older and younger females often give birth to a single cub. Triplets, while possible, are rare.

7. Male polar bears play no part in the daily lives of a mother and her cubs. After mating season, fathers leave and are never seen again.

8. Polar bear cubs are born with pink skin, but it turns black by their first birthdays.

9. "Grolar bear" or "pizzly"—these are the unofficial names given to the eight polar-bear-grizzly-bear hybrids discovered in the wild since 2006. All the pizzlies came from a single polar bear mother and two grizzly bear fathers. These hybrids look like a cross between the two species, with white fur interspersed with brown patches and a humped back like a grizzly

10. In the fall, hundreds of polar bears pass through Churchill, a town in Manitoba, as they make their way to the shore of Hudson Bay to wait for the return of ice. The people there have learned to live with the hungry bears. Doors aren't locked in case somebody has to make a quick escape, and patrols drive bears away from homes and businesses with sirens and air horns. For those bears that won't be scared off, Churchill has established a "polar bear jail." They trap or tranquilize the bear, then take it to a holding facility. When the bay freezes, the bear is taken by helicopter or vehicle onto the ice and released so it can continue its usual winter hunting routine.

POLAR BEARS ONLINE

Want to track Hudson Bay mothers and cubs in real time; watch bears sleep, eat, and play live on a "Polar Bear Cam"; or peek into a den? You can do all this and more at the website of Polar Bears International, the only conservation group dedicated solely to wild polar bears. Check it out at:

https://polarbearsinternational.org/

Looking for more? Then head over to the World Wildlife Fund site for facts, maps, photos and videos.
https://www.worldwildlife.org/species/polar-bear

And here's an episode from National Geographic's The Life of a Baby Polar Bear that has it all—tenderness, cuteness, suspense . . . and a wolf!
https://www.youtube.com/watch?v=9vgnXRypc4o

SELECTED BIBLIOGRAPHY

Derocher, Andrew E. *Polar Bears: A Complete Guide to Their Biology and Behavior.* Baltimore: Johns Hopkins University Press, 2012.

Krupnik, Igor and Aron L. Crowell, eds. *Arctic Crashes: People and Animals in the Changing North.* Washington, D.C.: Smithsonian Institution Scholarly Press, 2020.

Rawicki, Michel. *Polar Bears: A Life Under Threat.* New York, Acc Art Books, 2019.

Rosing, Norbert. *The World of the Polar Bear.* Richmond Hill, Ontario: Firefly Books, 2010.

Stirling, Ian. *Polar Bears: The Natural History of a Threatened Species.* Markham, Ontario: Fitzhenry & Whiteside, 2011.

Struzik, Ed. *Arctic Icons: How the Town of Churchill Learned to Love its Polar Bears.* Markham, Ontario: Fitzhenry & Whiteside, 2014.

ACKNOWLEDGMENTS

We are deeply indebted to Andrew E. Derocher, Ph.D., professor in the Department of Biological Sciences at the University of Alberta, Edmonton, Canada; editor-in-chief of *Ursus*, the journal of the International Association for Bear Research and Management; volunteer scientific advisor for Polar Bear International; and author of *Polar Bears: A Complete Guide to Their Biology and Behavior*, for vetting the text, as well as approving the illustrations. His vast knowledge of and lifetime commitment to polar bears is both extraordinary and inspiring.

To Ethan, for all you do.

Neal Porter Books

Text copyright © 2022 by Candace Fleming
Illustrations copyright © 2022 by Eric Rohmann
All Rights Reserved
HOLIDAY HOUSE is registered in the U.S. Patent and Trademark Office.
Printed and bound in July 2022 at Toppan Leefung, DongGuan, China.
The artwork for this book was made using oil paint on paper.
Book design by Jennifer Browne
www.holidayhouse.com
First Edition
10 9 8 7 6 5 4 3 2 1

Library of Congress Cataloging-in-Publication Data

Names: Fleming, Candace, author. | Rohmann, Eric, illustrator.
Title: Polar bear / Candace Fleming ; illustrated by Eric Rohmann.
Description: First edition. | New York : Holiday House, [2022] | Includes
    bibliographical references. | Audience: Ages 4 to 8 | Audience: Grades
    K–1 | Summary: "A book exploring the life and habitat of a mother polar
    bear and her cubs"— Provided by publisher.
Identifiers: LCCN 2022010443 | ISBN 9780823449163 (hardcover)
Subjects: LCSH: Polar bear—Juvenile literature. | Polar
    bear—Habitat—Juvenile literature.
Classification: LCC QL737.C27 F627 2022 | DDC 599.786—dc23/eng/20220420
LC record available at https://lccn.loc.gov/2022010443

ISBN 978-0-8234-4916-3 hardcover